The Financial Freedom Journal

Your growth guide for mastering money and transforming your life

DANIEL WHITE

This Journal Belongs To

....

Available in paperback and e-book
LCCN: 2023907177
ISBN: 978-1-63680-161-2 (paperback)
ISBN: 978-1-63680-162-9 (ebook)

DanielWhiteCoaching.com

DEDICATION

I dedicate this book to you and your commitment to overcoming the weaknesses and limitations you have created in your relationship with money.

With consistency and perseverance, you will look back in a few years and marvel at how free your life is now that your relationship with money has been transformed.

Enjoy the Journey!

To your Freedom

Daniel White

CONTENTS

1. Using This Journal 1

Section One

2. Your Personal Commitment to Financial Freedom................... 5
3. The 7 Steps Simplified.. 6
4. Step 1 - Decide and Commit... 8
5. Step 2 - Envision a Full Tank... 9
6. Step 3 - Calculate Reality..10
7. Step 4 - Deposit at the Bank...12
8. Your Financial Freedom Scorecard...................................14
9. Your Life Transformations 28
10. Transforming Your Habits 30
11. Step 5 - Grow and Protect 34
12. Step 6 - Reach and Go Beyond Your Critical Mass.................36
13. Building Your Three Month's Supply................................38
14. Step 7 - Enjoy Life...43
15. Celebrating Your Wins..44
16. Beyond Your Transformational Goal.................................48

Section Two

17. Your Freedom Journal Pages..53
18. About the Author..115
19. Contact Daniel White...117

USING THIS JOURNAL

This journal is designed to be a practical companion to The Financial Freedom System book. It is divided into two parts:

1. The first provides a brief overview of the key concepts outlined in the 7 Steps of The Financial Freedom System, as well as action Checklists and Scorecards to be completed as you work your way through the system.

2. The second contains Your Freedom Journal Pages where you can explore and write your insights and experiences throughout your transformational journey to financial freedom.

All the activities and exercises you need to complete as part of the process are included in the first section. So, work your way through each step, paying attention to your inner responses and self-talk, and use this journal as a powerful tool to record and reflect on your progress.

The information and insights you will most benefit from recording in your journal are:

- Using Your Freedom Scorecard to record the weekly deposits you make as well as the total balance in your Foundation Account at the beginning of each month. This journal contains enough of these scorecards to record three years of monthly amounts.

- The positive thoughts and feelings you have as you make your deposits and see your Foundation Account growing. Also, to record any ego, arrogance, and negative chatter which is exposed while following this system. Notice how you react to the situation as you make your deposits, observe your thoughts and record these in your journal. This will reveal any weaknesses in your Foundation.

- Limiting beliefs and negative money habits which you wish to clear from your consciousness can be listed and written about in Your Transformation Scorecards. By bringing your awareness to these ego-based patterns, they will begin to transform and clear. Reach out if you want to join a Group Transformation Session with Daniel to gain further insight on how to shift these patterns or receive a healing to clear the issues.

- If you become frustrated by slow progress in the first few months of using this system, remember to breathe! This is only a test to see if you're serious about transforming your life. *Measure back* to where you were at the start of your journey and realize that if you had not have started the Financial Freedom System, you wouldn't have any of the money you've collected in your Foundation Account. See this as a significant improvement in your life. Record your insights in your Freedom Journal Pages.

- Start noticing and recording the 'wins' and positive results of your new weekly habits in your finances and other areas of your life. Record these notes in your Celebration Scorecard.

- Acknowledge and appreciate how much you've grown by following this system, and remember to enjoy this life-changing transformational journey. Your future self will be so grateful that you did.

So, let's get started.

SECTION ONE

What would you feel with 100 percent of your annual income in your bank account?

YOUR PERSONAL COMMITMENT
TO FINANCIAL FREEDOM

Begin your financial freedom journey today and commit to the process by answering these simple questions: (If you have already completed this in your copy of The Financial Freedom System book, transfer your figures into the journal now.)

When will you commence The Financial Freedom System—today, tomorrow, this week, or this month? Enter your start date here:

....

....

....

What is your greatest reason for committing to The Financial Freedom System? Your *why* will support your 100-percent rock-solid commitment. Please write your reason for commitment here:

....

....

....

What is your current annual income?

Before Taxes: ....

After Taxes: ....

THE 7 STEPS SIMPLIFIED

Below is a quick overview of the 7 Steps of the Financial Freedom System and beyond. This will give you a brief refresher and empower you to get started today.

Stop Digging!

To start your journey to financial peace of mind and abundance, you must stop digging a financial hole. Stop trying to find get-rich-quick ways out of your financial situation and commit to building your financial foundation. Your path to financial freedom lies in the transformational process of building your Foundation Account. Your Foundation Account is where you make weekly deposits based upon the level of growth in your unconscious at that time. These deposits build solid, secure steps upward out of your financial hole on your journey from scarcity to abundance.

Steps 1 to 4 – You stop digging your financial hole by changing your habits with a strong intention. Follow the first 4 Steps of The Financial Freedom System:

Step 1: Decide and Commit to the Financial Freedom System. Remember, deciding is making a choice above the neck; committing is taking action below the neck.

Step 2: Envision a Full Tank and create a clear vision of the transformation you'll experience by building your Foundation. This gives you the all-important initial energy to take ongoing physical action toward achieving your goal.

Step 3: Calculate Reality by calculating your initial deposit amount. This amount needs to be real for you and not inflated by your ego or others' influences. Choose an amount for your weekly deposit that fits into your current budget and doesn't cause you financial stress.

Step 4: Deposit at the Bank and begin building your Foundation Account. Each time you make a deposit, you'll experience an increased level of energy and peace.

Once you have completed Step 4 and made your initial deposit, you have reached your first Freedom Breakthrough; **integrity.**

Step 5: Grow and Protect - Once you have calculated the increased amount of your weekly deposit, you have reached your next Freedom Breakthrough; **intuition.**

Step 6: Reach and Go Beyond Your Critical Mass – On the completion of The 12 Month Test, you have reached and gone beyond your Critical Mass. This marks your third Freedom Breakthrough; **mastery and respect.**

Step 7: Enjoy Life – Continue building your Foundation until you reach the goal of having 100 percent of your original annual income, before taxes, in your account.

Beyond Your Transformational Goal – You set a new transformational goal to reach the level of 100 percent of your new current annual income in your Foundation Account. Continue building your Foundation until you reach this amount.

Congratulations!

Following are the action Checklists for each Step.

STEP 1 - DECIDE AND COMMIT

All growth starts with taking action below the neck. If you want something to change in your life, simply thinking about it, talking about it, or visualizing it won't change anything. You also have to take inspired *action*. In Step 1, you are asked to **decide** and **commit** to the Financial Freedom System. Remember, deciding is making a choice above the neck; committing is taking action below the neck.

Step 1 Checklist

- **Decide** to transform your life into a new experience of freedom, peace, and abundance. To strengthen your decision, recognize that you are also choosing to overcome perceived *weaknesses* in the area of finances and money management. Every day, say out loud with conviction, "I choose to create financial freedom in my life." Write this statement on a sticky note, and place it where you will see it daily.

- **Commit** to taking action below the neck, beginning on the date you chose in *Your Personal Commitment to Financial Freedom section.* Then decide which day of the week you're going to make your deposits. I recommend Monday mornings to train your unconscious to pay yourself first every week.

- **Take Action** by writing down your answers to the questions in the Your Personal Commitment section in this journal.

- **Record** details about your transformational journey to build your Foundation, including weekly deposit amounts, monthly Foundation totals, monthly increase amounts, thoughts, feelings, and insights using your scorecards and Freedom Journal Pages.

STEP 2 - ENVISION A FULL TANK

Having a clear vision of the transformation, you'll experience by building your Foundation is essential. This gives you the all-important initial energy to take ongoing physical action toward achieving your goal. Therefore, it is essential to *see your financial tank as full* in Step 2.

Step 2 Checklist

- **Acknowledge** how much you have in your bank account right now.

- **Check in** with yourself and ask, "What do I feel about my current balance?" Write down your thoughts here.

....

- **Visualize** having the equivalent of 100 percent of your annual income, before taxes, in your bank account.

- **Check-in again.** What do you feel about your projected balance? Write this down here.

....

- **Compare** the two feelings. Which feeling do you prefer and why?

For most people, the image of having a full tank makes them feel more relaxed and less burdened with stress.

STEP 3 - CALCULATE REALITY

Your next step is to calculate the deposit amount necessary to start building your Foundation Account. This amount needs to be *real* for you and not inflated by your ego or others' influences. Choose an amount for your weekly deposit that fits into your current budget and doesn't cause you financial stress. Your correct deposit amount is one you won't miss in your present financial situation. In Step 3, you need to *Calculate Reality* based on your current financial situation.

Step 3 Checklist

- **Ask** God to strengthen your intuition so you can gain the best results for your deposit amount. Partnering with God also helps you overcome your ego.

- **Calculate** mentally (above the neck). Work out your whole financial situation and budget. Then think of an amount you will be able to handle as your deposit and not miss from your finances each week.

If the amount creates stress and tension in your body, then it's too high. You can start with any amount—50 cents, $1, $10, or $20. It doesn't matter; what's important is that you feel at ease with your amount. As you deposit the money and your unconscious energy shifts, the amount you can comfortably deposit will grow. Before you can get there, you must establish integrity with your present reality. (I even had a wealthy client who started with just 25 cents each week.)

- **Calculate** emotionally (below the neck). See yourself depositing this amount each week. Does your body feel relaxed? If not, lower the amount until you feel at ease. Don't build your financial Foundation with your ego, or it will fall apart like a house of cards when the strong winds of life blow your way. Also, do not, under any circumstances, compare the amount of your deposit with your annual income, as this will create stress.

STEP 4 - DEPOSIT AT THE BANK

It's now time to begin building your Foundation by making your first deposit in Step 4. Each time you make a deposit, you'll experience an increased level of energy and peace. At first, you might find the energy shifts are subtle, depending on how deeply embedded your old habits have become. However, over time, greater energy and peace will come as your unconscious is transformed. Much like when you plant a seed in the ground, it may take a few weeks before you see visible signs of growth appear above ground.

Step 4 Checklist

- **Open** your Foundation Account at the bank. Find an account that doesn't attract high fees at a location where you can make your deposits in person or through the ATM, as opposed to online.

- **Make your deposits** in person. You must make your Foundation Account deposit with *your own hands*. Having someone else do it for you won't work, and neither will making the deposit by electronic transfer. Only you can transform your unconscious and develop your new financial habits. That is why you must physically take your deposits to the bank.

- **Check in** with your feelings. As you make each deposit, notice how you react to the situation and be aware of the thoughts that arise. This will reveal any weaknesses in your Foundation.

- **Record** Use your Freedom Scorecard to record your weekly deposits, monthly totals, and increase amounts, and write about your insights in the Freedom Journal Pages as you continue to build your Foundation.

Once you have completed Steps 1 through 4 and made your initial deposit, you have reached your first Freedom Breakthrough; **integrity.**

At this point in the transformation of your relationship with money and finances, the key is to be in a state of integrity with your deposit calculation and to take inspired action. Be truly sincere with this step in the process, as it will strengthen your results for your future.

As you continue to make deposits into your Foundation Account, remember to acknowledge your progress with this step:

- **Celebrate** each month to honor how much your Foundation has grown since you started making your deposits as a way of acknowledging your progress. Record your thoughts and wins in the Celebration Scorecard.

YOUR FINANCIAL FREEDOM SCORECARD

- Record the deposit amounts for each month of your journey. This journal has enough pages for the first three years of deposits.

- Add a checkmark for each week the deposit has been made to record your progress.

- Record the amount of accumulated funds in your Foundation Account at the beginning of each month.

- As you make your deposit, notice how you react. Observe how you feel physically if emotions arise, and remain mindful of your thoughts. This will reveal any weaknesses in your foundation. If there are any limiting beliefs, negative patterns, or issues you would like to overcome, record them in Your Transformation Scorecards. You can also join one of our Group Transformation Sessions or reach out to Daniel for a clearing to transform these weaknesses into strengths.

- Write down any insights you have at each stage of your journey in Your Freedom Pages.

- Record the wins, positive thoughts, and feelings you have as you make your deposits and see your Foundation Account grow. Also, write down any ego, arrogance, and negative chatter that gets exposed while following this system.

- If you become frustrated by slow progress in the first few months of using this system, remember to breathe! Refer to the breathing exercise in the Financial Freedom System book. This is only a test to see if you're serious about transforming your life. *Measure back* to where you were at the start of your journey and realize that if you had not started this process, you wouldn't have any of the money you've collected in your Foundation Account. See this as a significant improvement in your life.

Financial Freedom Scorecard

Month and Year	Check mark after completing each weekly deposit	Weekly Deposit Amount for this Month	Accumulated Total of Foundation Account at the beginning of the Month
July, 2022	✓ ✓ ✓	$35	$1,395

Financial Freedom Scorecard

Any Insights for this month's deposit amount that stand out to you?	Your Wins and Positive thoughts and feelings from this month's deposits	Ego, Arrogance and negative chatter you noticed during this month
After increasing the deposit $5 this month, I felt more grounded each week.	*There is a firmness and commitment each time I made a deposit. There is no question that this is a transformation for the rest of my life.*	*When I was shopping for a shirt the other day, the sales rep was pushing me to buy a style that didn't feel good with and in my mind, I started doubting myself.*

Financial Freedom Scorecard

Month and Year	Check mark after completing each weekly deposit	Weekly Deposit Amount for this Month	Accumulated Total of Foundation Account at the beginning of the Month

Financial Freedom Scorecard

Any Insights for this month's deposit amount that stand out to you?	Your Wins and Positive thoughts and feelings from this month's deposits	Ego, Arrogance and negative chatter you noticed during this month

Financial Freedom Scorecard

Month and Year	Check mark after completing each weekly deposit	Weekly Deposit Amount for this Month	Accumulated Total of Foundation Account at the beginning of the Month

Financial Freedom Scorecard

Any Insights for this month's deposit amount that stand out to you?	Your Wins and Positive thoughts and feelings from this month's deposits	Ego, Arrogance and negative chatter you noticed during this month

Financial Freedom Scorecard

Month and Year	Check mark after completing each weekly deposit	Weekly Deposit Amount for this Month	Accumulated Total of Foundation Account at the beginning of the Month

Financial Freedom Scorecard

Any Insights for this month's deposit amount that stand out to you?	Your Wins and Positive thoughts and feelings from this month's deposits	Ego, Arrogance and negative chatter you noticed during this month

Financial Freedom Scorecard

Month and Year	Check mark after completing each weekly deposit	Weekly Deposit Amount for this Month	Accumulated Total of Foundation Account at the beginning of the Month

Financial Freedom Scorecard

Any Insights for this month's deposit amount that stand out to you?	Your Wins and Positive thoughts and feelings from this month's deposits	Ego, Arrogance and negative chatter you noticed during this month

Financial Freedom Scorecard

Month and Year	Check mark after completing each weekly deposit	Weekly Deposit Amount for this Month	Accumulated Total of Foundation Account at the beginning of the Month

Financial Freedom Scorecard

Any Insights for this month's deposit amount that stand out to you?	Your Wins and Positive thoughts and feelings from this month's deposits	Ego, Arrogance and negative chatter you noticed during this month

YOUR LIFE TRANSFORMATIONS

- Here you can list any of the limiting beliefs and behaviors you would like to transform in regards to your finances.

- As you follow the system, you will become aware of these limitations in your daily life. If you notice that you are becoming conscious of the behavior, add it to the Transformation Scorecard below.

- As your Foundation Account builds over time, record the dates when you first notice that you have transformed a limiting belief. This will be evident when you find they no longer have any power over you and your behavior has changed.

- If you would like help with these blockages, reach out to Daniel to find out when the next group transformation session (GTS) is to eliminate these permanently.

Life Transformations

Date:	Limiting belief to work on:	Date transformed:
Example: *July 2022*	*I never have enough money, I'm always broke*	*August 2022*

TRANSFORMING YOUR HABITS

- Throughout your Financial Freedom journey you will be letting go of old money habits and replacing them with new ones.

- This scorecard is designed as a place for you to become conscious of old and outdated ways of being and to begin to create new habits based upon your integrity, intuition, mastery and respect for your financial Foundation.

- As you look at this Habit Transformation Scorecard during your journey, you will gain energy seeing how much you have grown and transformed.

Habit Transformations

Date:	Negative habits that have changed in your life	How much have you grown? Write it down here
Aug 2022	*Over-spending and getting into debt*	*I now use cash to pay for my purchases and live within my means, so I can repay my debts.*

Habit Transformations

Date:	Negative habits that have changed in your life	How much have you grown? Write it down here

Habit Transformations

Date:	Negative habits that have changed in your life	How much have you grown? Write it down here

STEP 5 - GROW AND PROTECT

In Step 5 you are building your way out of your financial hole and growing towards your Critical Mass. Here you build your Foundation Account and increase inner peace. Remember to stick to the system and maintain your weekly deposits and monthly increases. If you try to get out of the hole too fast by short-cutting the system, you will only find yourself digging another hole. Once you have completed Step 5, and calculated your deposit increase, you have reached your next Freedom Breakthrough: **intuition.**

With this step you are developing a deeper relationship with your intuition, where it grows to become stronger than your ego. Using your intuition in this way enables you to stay strong and remain below the neck as your financial consciousness expands. Therefore, the transformation of this next breakthrough is that it profoundly develops your intuition with money and your finances.

Step 5 Checklist

- **Reflect** each month on how much you can grow your weekly deposit without feeling stress. Make sure the amount is not more than double the previous month's deposit, regardless of how strong you feel. Do the breathing exercise before you calculate the deposit increase to keep ego from influencing your decision.

- **Protect** yourself by being mindful of your ego's attempts to stop, slow down, or sabotage the process. Ignore the thought that says, "*This method doesn't work.*" Don't overspend because your ego says, "*I really need and deserve this new toy!*" This is blatant self-sabotage. Use your Financial Freedom Journal to record the progress you have achieved since you started the system and to write about any ego interferences along your journey.

- **Breathe** your way to financial freedom. Every time you make a deposit into your Foundation Account or jar, do the two-minute breathing process as described in the Financial Freedom System before, during, and after making your deposit.

- **Record** your results, and also notice habits in other areas of your life. Put these notes into your Freedom and Transformation Scorecards.

- **Check-in** with your feelings. Each month, repeat the visualization of your current bank balance and imagine your annual income in your Foundation Account. Record any changes in how you feel about your current bank account balance in your journal pages.

The Critical Mass Illusion

Warning! Once you have built your Foundation to a point where you have raised yourself partly out of your financial hole, you may *think* you have mastered money and reached your Critical Mass. **Be Careful! Only your eyes are only seeing *out of your financial hole, above ground*. The rest of your body is still in the financial hole.** The Critical Mass Illusion is where the ego tries to trick you into thinking that you have made it. In my experience, it takes at least another 12 months of weekly deposits to finally stabilize your Foundation and get you completely out of your financial hole.

STEP 6 - REACH AND GO BEYOND YOUR CRITICAL MASS

Reaching your Critical Mass and then passing this level means that you have now dug yourself out of your financial hole in Step 6. By completing The 12 Month Test you have now passed your next Freedom Breakthrough; **mastery and respect.** During this time you have also built up your three months' supply of non-perishable goods at home and paid your mortgage or rent three months in advance.

This is the most important breakthrough in your progress through The Financial Freedom System and will impact your life in a multitude of profound ways. The steps you took to achieve the earlier breakthroughs have brought you to the tipping point in your journey. You have undergone a transformation in your unconscious, just as coal under pressure transforms into a diamond. At this stage, you live in **integrity** with your finances, your **intuition** is strong and clear and you can consciously choose how best to manage and utilize your money. You have gained **respect** for your finances and become **the master of money,** in return you are more attractive to money and opportunities in life. You have learned the key lessons of the system at this point and taken your life to a new level!

Step 6 Checklist

- **Continue to build** your Foundation Account until you reach and go beyond your Critical Mass.
- **Stay focused with your deposits** for an additional 12 months to solidify your Critical Mass strength, and complete The 12 Month Test.

- **Strengthen your position** by building three months' worth of supplies at home. Use your extra money each month to buy three months' supply of one non-perishable item at a time. Then move on to the second item, and so on. Use the Three Month's Supply Scorecard below to record your growth as you build the supplies of non-perishable goods in your home.

- **Check your results,** acknowledging how much you've grown by following this system. Write down your results in your Freedom and Transformation Scorecards and record your insights in the Freedom Pages. If you are happy to share your successes, contact us as we would love to hear your stories.

- **Experience the feeling** of how much more relaxed you are, even when you have no money in your pocket. Peace, stability, and emotional freedom come from the power of building a strong Foundation for yourself. Enjoy!

BUILDING YOUR THREE MONTH'S SUPPLY

During your 12 Month Test, strengthen your Foundation by purchasing three month's-worth of non-perishable items for your home. To calculate how much you will need, consider how much of this item you and your family use each month. Then multiply this amount by a factor of three to arrive at your three month's supply figure.

Each week, you can slowly build your supplies by choosing to purchase enough of one or two items to last you for three months. In this way you can work your way through a list of all items that you use in a three month period.

Your non-perishable items will include tinned, dried and packaged foods, cooking needs, other products found in your pantry, kitchen, bathroom, laundry, home office, garage or garden. Also consider health supplements, medications, batteries, light bulbs, matches, pet related products, cleaning items, car supplies and any other miscellaneous products you use.

Three Month's Supply Record

Date:	Non-Perishable Items	Three Month's Supply Amounts	Date Achieved	1 year later, what are the new three month supply amounts?	2 years later, what are the new three month supply amounts?	3 years later, what are the new three month supply amounts?
Aug 2022	Toilet Paper	30 rolls	September 2022	2023 down to 25 rolls.	2024	2025

Three Month's Supply Record

Date:	Non-Perishable Items	Three Month's Supply Amounts	Date Achieved	1 year later, what are the new three month supply amounts?	2 years later, what are the new three month supply amounts?	3 years later, what are the new three month supply amounts?

Three Month's Supply Record

Date:	Non-Perishable Items	Three Month's Supply Amounts	Date Achieved	1 year later, what are the new three month supply amounts?	2 years later, what are the new three month supply amounts?	3 years later, what are the new three month supply amounts?

Three Month's Supply Record

Date:	Non-Perishable Items	Three Month's Supply Amounts	Date Achieved	1 year later, what are the new three month supply amounts?	2 years later, what are the new three month supply amounts?	3 years later, what are the new three month supply amounts?

STEP 7 - ENJOY LIFE

During Step 7, you grow your Foundation Account from your Critical Mass to 100-percent of your original annual income. Stay committed and disciplined to reach this transformational goal. Keep following the steps, making the weekly deposits and growing your Foundation Account until you reach the important goal you established when you started The Financial Freedom System.

Step 7 Checklist

- **Reach 100-percent** by increasing your weekly deposits until you achieve the equivalent of your original annual income, before taxes, no matter how many years it takes!

- **Monitor money flow**. Each year monitor the changes in your income and expenses so you're consciously aware of the dynamics of how money flows through your life.

- **Acknowledge and celebrate** the achievement of the goal you set at the beginning of your lifetime transformational process.

- **Record** your personal wins, positive results and unexpected financial outcomes in the Celebration Scorecard below. Acknowledging and celebrating the increased abundance and new levels of prosperity in your life forms an important part of the transformational process.

- **Write in your journal**, describing your feelings and experiences of achieving this massive goal and the journey you took to get here. If you would like to share your journey with me and my team, please contact us—details are in the back of this book.

CELEBRATING YOUR WINS

- List any financial or personal wins which have occurred since you commenced The Financial Freedom System in the scorecard below. These can include increases in income, extra money flowing into your life, spending less money, receiving unexpected cash or lump sums, gifts, opportunities, travel or positive new conditions or relationships in any area of your life.

- Explain whether they were expected or unexpected. Also reflect upon why and how you received these outcomes.

- Record how you felt, physically, emotionally, mentally and spiritually.

Celebration Scorecard

Date	My Wins and Positive Outcomes	How did you feel and what happened?
Jan 2023	I received an unexpected lump sum of cash	A relative left me an unexpected inheritance and I received $50,000 I felt deep gratitude and joy, yet I did not become over excited.

Celebration Scorecard

Date	My Wins and Positive Outcomes	How did you feel and what happened?

Celebration Scorecard

Date	My Wins and Positive Outcomes	How did you feel and what happened?

BEYOND YOUR TRANSFORMATIONAL GOAL

As it has taken time to build your Foundation Account over a few years, your annual income will have increased. Now you are ready to move to the next level of stability.

Your New Current Annual Income Goal

Once you have reached 100-percent of your original annual income amount, you will have transformed your level of consciousness. This is an impactful part of the process. Now that you have achieved 100-percent of your original annual income goal and your tank is full, what is your next move?

Your next goal is to build your Foundation to a greater level of stability.

What is your new current annual income now that you have reached 100-percent of your starting annual income?

Please write your new current annual income below.

Amount: ....

This becomes your new Foundation goal.

Keep making deposits into your Foundation Account until you make up the difference between the two annual income amounts. This will happen much faster than it did with your previous amount.

Once you reach the level of 100-percent of your new current annual income in your Foundation Account, you have completed this process.

On what date did you reach 100% of your new current annual income?

Date Achieved: ....

Congratulations!

With 100-percent of your new annual income in your Foundation Account, you have now transformed your financial consciousness for the future. You have completed all 7 steps and are now standing on solid financial ground.

SECTION TWO

That which is measured, recorded, and reflected upon transforms exponentially.

YOUR FREEDOM JOURNAL PAGES

This section of the Financial Freedom Journal is dedicated as space for you to write about your innermost reflections, insights, and thoughts on the transformational process you experience. Feel free to express yourself with words, sketches, and freehand diagrams, if you are drawn to do so. The pages have been intentionally left blank, with a simple quote at the bottom of each page, so your creativity can flow.

Record your Results - You may wish to write about your personal experiences and events which occur. Or you may begin to observe shifts in your results or weekly habits in other areas of your life. Write these notes into your Freedom Journal Pages to record your transformation and breakthrough moments.

Reflect and Acknowledge – Think about how much you've grown through following The Financial Freedom System. Write down how you feel physically, mentally, emotionally, and spiritually about your results, and describe inspiring moments and any shifts in behavior or habits for which you are grateful.

Enjoy Yourself – Know that you are transforming yourself financially and in all other areas of your life. So, enjoy the journey and use the Foundation Journal Pages as a practical and empowering tool for growth.

Here's to your success!

*Begin your journey to become
financially free today.*

Put the oxygen mask on yourself
first before you help others.

You can start with any deposit amount—$1.00, $10.00, or $20.00, it doesn't matter—what's important is that you feel at ease with your amount.

Different money energy =
Different money habits

This is not about getting rich quickly, instead, it's about becoming wealthy for life.

Building a strong Financial Foundation will allow life to flow for you, not against you.

Principle 1- Reconnecting with God: Your 100-percent commitment will give you strength, and close any gaps where fear or doubt can sneak in and sabotage your goal.

Principle 2 - Trusting Your Intuition:
When you follow your intuition, life flows
for you. When you pray or speak with God,
your intuition is God answering you.

*Principle 3 – Protecting Your Environment:
When you protect your home and
environment from negative influences,
you remain clear and grounded.*

Principle 4 – Leading Yourself into Action:
You become the master of your life as a
whole by first mastering your ego, habits,
unconscious patterns, and, of course, money.

Savers respect their money and work to create wealth and security over the long term.

Pay yourself first before you spend elsewhere.

It is critical to your success to first know what is real for you today before you begin your journey to building your Foundation.

All growth happens by taking action below the neck. Deciding is above the neck, and committing is below the neck.

*Power is created by deciding on a
course of action and then committing
to following through on it.*

*When babies are learning to walk, they
keep falling down but get back up again
and again. They don't give up by thinking,
"This walking thing is not for me."*

*The creation of a strong Foundation
is key to your success in life.*

Being unconscious about your income (before and after taxes) is like not wearing your oxygen mask in a plane when it's losing air pressure. It will suck the money right out of your life.

*Three years from now, what do you
wish you had started today?*

Your awareness of your intuition will increase as you build your Foundation, and the stress will leave your mind and body.

Before you can transform any area of your life, you must first accept where you are here and now. Your current reality is the starting point to plan your future journey.

Remind yourself of your goal every day with this statement, "I choose to create financial freedom in my life."

Be careful not to compare your deposit amount to your annual income, because it will focus your mind on lack and where you are now, instead of transformation, freedom, and where you want to be.

It's not the size of your deposit that matters—it is the consistent action and growth that transforms you and your life.

As you deposit the money and your unconscious energy begins to shift, the amount you can deposit will grow.

Inner contentment and peace build security,
enabling you to move towards a better, more
creative, productive, and fulfilling life.

Your weekly deposits must be made in person and in cash.

Read through The Financial Freedom System book every month for the first year until the habits becomes solid, then at least once a year after that, to remind yourself of the principles.

Each time you make a deposit,
you'll experience an increased level
of energy and inner peace.

Just like when you plant a seed in the ground, it may take a few weeks before you see the visible signs of growth. When it finally breaks through the ground, you will see the shoots coming up from under the earth.

When you look back in a few years, you'll see how much you have grown, which will give you a sense of achievement and satisfaction as you move towards your lifetime transformation goal.

*Ask yourself, "Have I paid
myself first this week?"*

*With each month you progress, you'll
look forward to the next month's
increase and notice a sense of happiness,
strength, and positivity running
through your mind and body.*

*Be stronger than your excuses
and stay the course.*

Remember, it's the action of making the deposit yourself that transforms your unconscious and builds the Foundation for your future. It's not the amount you deposit.

As you build your Foundation and your unconscious starts letting go of old limiting beliefs, you become more stable and relaxed and won't feel the need to spend as much on food, entertainment, or toys.

You will become more attractive to money because of your new respect for it and for yourself.

Don't let your frustrations take you backwards, instead let them grow you towards your goals.

One of the greatest lessons I learned in my career as a runner was to have goals to aim for and to measure back to see how I was improving.

*Experience the breakthrough transformation
you feel in your body as you achieve your
Critical Mass level. Enthusiasm and
confidence become the new normal, along
with increased levels of energy and peace.*

A welcome side benefit of reaching and passing your Critical Mass is that you will find you consistently have extra money left over at the end of each month.

Once you feel you have reached your Critical Mass level, see this as the starting point for the 12-month test. Keep focused on the process for the next 12 months and if the great feeling is consistent for the whole year, you know you have really made it!

Having your Critical Mass in the bank is like driving your car, knowing that you have plenty of fuel in the tank

*The peace, stability and freedom from
stress you will feel comes from the power of
building a strong Foundation for yourself.*

*When you have built a solid
Foundation, you have created a
launch pad for the rest of your life.*

Keep building your Foundation until you reach the goal of having 100-percent of your original annual income in your account.

Once you have reached the goal of having your annual income in your Foundation Account, you will know that you have mastered your finances and your habits around spending and receiving.

You'll notice more energy and more income moving towards you. You will also have developed a deep respect for the energy of money.

Each year monitor the changes in your income and expenses so you're consciously aware of how money flows through your life.

Celebrate the achievement of your
Foundation Account goal.

You will experience the feeling of having an overflow of abundance.

Now that you have achieved 100-percent of your annual income goal and your tank is full, what is your next step?

Once you go beyond 100-percent of your annual income, you have more control over your spending and your finances. At this level, advertising and the media have a great deal less power over you and your spending decisions.

Taking money out of your Foundation Account to pay for problems in your life will cause weaknesses in your financial stability and in your energy. Do whatever you can to maintain the integrity of your Foundation.

*Remember to keep moving forward and
do not stop building your Foundation.*

Once you have created this new set of habits with money, you will create a totally different reality in your life.

The real value of this system goes well beyond money. It's about living from a genuine experience of abundance that will show up in your well-being, your relationships and in the way you approach life.

With 100-percent of your new annual income in your Foundation Account, you have now transformed your financial consciousness for the future. You are now standing on solid financial ground.

If humanity had the consciousness of security and abundance, there'd be a massive increase in contribution, and a decrease in the amount of stress and illness in people's lives. The world would be a happier place in which to live.

We need to be able to hold the energy of abundance, so that our body, our mind, and our consciousness have the chance to accept abundance as normal – and not spend our energy and money on trying to escape from our fears!

Perhaps the most profound impact of The Financial Freedom System is the spiritual transformation you will experience once you fully complete the seven steps outlined in my system.

ABOUT THE AUTHOR

Daniel (Kim) White has been consulting since 1994 and has worked with clients in over forty countries. Recognized internationally for his unique intuitive gifts, he is a sought-after speaker and author. He works closely with his clients to help them overcome energetic blockages to abundance and financial freedom, empowering them to create a better future for themselves, their families, and their businesses.

Daniel's own struggles with finances inspired him to find a transformational solution that enabled him to build his financial freedom. He searched for answers about how financial habits and behaviors, as well as external energetic influences, can affect finances. The answers he discovered and the processes he developed during this search made his work and its results powerfully transformative. That's why he created The Financial Freedom System and teaches the 7 Steps to clients around the world.

Originally from Perth, Western Australia, Daniel has a bachelor's degree in business administration from Northern Arizona University, where he attended on an athletic scholarship while training for selection in the 1992 Australian Olympic team. He continues to improve his ability to assist clients to transform their energy, environments, and relationships. He lives and works globally, still runs for fitness as well as pleasure, and enjoys great coffee and wonderful food with friends.

CONTACT DANIEL WHITE

I would like to hear from you if you want to know more about any of the following:

- Connecting with me to learn more about my coaching services
- Accessing further ways for you to strengthen your Foundation
- Joining my online Group Transformation Sessions
- Receiving regular newsletters and invitations to upcoming events
- Sharing your Financial Freedom stories and experiences
- Purchasing your copy of The Financial Freedom System book
- Continuing your financial journey by graduating to the next level

Email Daniel or the team at: daniel@danielwhitecoaching.com

DanielWhiteCoaching.com

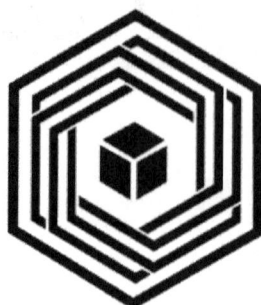

BLOCKCHAIN
VERIFIED IP™

Powered by Easy IP™

www.ingramcontent.com/pod-product-compliance
Lightning Source LLC
Chambersburg PA
CBHW071428210326
41597CB00020B/3701